LIONS & CHEETAHS & RHINOS OH MY!

Animal Artwork by Children in Sub-Saharan Africa

By John Platt and Moira Rose Donohue

PUBLISHED BY SLEEPING BEAR PRESS

Do you like wild animals?

Would you like to paint one?

How about a LION?

You should first start by drawing one. Look closely. But don't get too close! The lion is a ferocious hunter. At night, it can see eight times better than you can. Oh my! Perhaps you should start with a gentler African animal, like a . . .

Artist: Christopher, Malawi

ZEBRA.

Artist: Christopher, Malawi

The zebra looks like a horse in striped pajamas. The stripes are vertical (up and down) on the main part of the animal's body, but they go sideways on its rump!

Zebras often travel in herds. You can tell them apart because the pattern of each zebra's stripes is different, like fingerprints. But if you get tired of drawing stripes, you could draw something with spots, like a . . .

Artists: Elizabeth, Tanzania; Raymondi, Tanzania

CHEETAH.

Artist: Samuel, Kenya

The cheetah is smaller than a lion and has distinctive black spots on its yellow coat to help it hide in the golden grass of the African plains.

But you better draw fast before it dashes away. The cheetah is the fastest animal on land. It can race at 65 miles per hour (105 kilometers per hour) when chasing a meal. If you want to draw some bigger spots, you could draw a . . .

Artist: Rahim, Tanzania

GIRAFFE.

Artists: Lerato, Malawi

It's covered in spots, too. Like the zebra's stripes, the pattern of spots on the giraffe's fur is special to each animal.

The giraffe is the tallest animal on earth. It's as tall as three basketball players standing on each other's heads. Giraffes often sleep standing up—usually for only five minutes at a time. These gentle creatures feast on flowers and leaves. Want to draw another animal that loves its vegetables? How about a . . .

Artists: Lerato, Malawi; Yohani, Tanzania

RHINOCEROS!

Like giraffes, rhinos eat leaves and tender bushes.
But they eat plants that grow closer to the ground!

Artist: Naomi, Tanzania

Some rhinos have only one horn. But these are African rhinos. They have two horns on their noses. If you like drawing horns, you could draw an . . .

IMPALA.

The impala is a type of antelope. Male impalas have a pair of Y-shaped horns that they use to fight over who is in charge of a territory.

Impalas have short tails and black markings on their rear that form the shape of the letter M. Or you could draw another animal with a short tail, like the . . .

HIPPOPOTAMUS.

The hippo stays cool under the hot Africa sun by taking long baths. Sometimes bath time can last all day. But the hippo is happy in the water. It's a cousin to the whale!

Artist: Lerato, Malawi

At night, the hippo trudges out of the water to feed on grass. Hippos have long teeth that they show off by opening their mouths very wide, like this one! But if you don't want to draw a hippo, how about another night prowler? You could draw a . . .

LEOPARD.

Artist: Vicenti, Tanzania

The leopard is the largest spotted cat in Africa. Its round spots are called rosettes.

But it may be hard to find a leopard, as they are shy. You can sometimes spot one in a tree by looking for its dangling tail or its bright blue or green eyes. Can't find a leopard? That's okay. Look for something big, like a . . .

POLAR BEAR.

No, polar bears don't live in Africa!

Artist: Christopher, Malawi

But GORILLAS do.

Some gorillas inhabit the lush, tropical forests of western sub-Saharan Africa. Others hang out in the mountains of Central Africa.

The gorilla is the largest of the group of animals called primates. Humans are primates, too. Like humans, the gorilla has arms, legs, fingers, and toes; but it usually walks on all fours!

But if the gorilla isn't big enough for you, how about something even bigger?

Something like an . . .

Artist: Penuel, Kenya

ELEPHANT.

Artist: Yohani, Tanzania

The elephant is the world's largest land mammal. The African elephant has giant ears that flap back and forth, and beautiful ivory tusks. Elephants use their tusks to protect themselves and to find food.

Elephants are so gigantic that they have to eat and drink all day. They use their long trunks to suck up water to spray into their mouths. An elephant can drink 50 gallons (189 liters) a day. That's 800 glasses of water!

But you still want to draw a lion? Of course you do!

The LION

is regal—the king of beasts. It's a symbol of pride and strength in many African cultures. A male lion's head is surrounded by long, dark fur called a mane. He protects the female and young lions in his family, which is called a pride.

Artist: Christopher, Malawi

The female lions raise the lion cubs and are the primary hunters for the pride.

An animal this majestic inspires everyone. Let's all draw a lion and then paint it!

Artist: Yohani, Tanzania

There are many more beautiful animals in Africa—birds, snakes, monkeys, wildebeest, and even crocodiles. You can paint any animal you want. Or you can paint them all!

Sadly, many of these animals are endangered and may die out. Animal lives are being lost each day to conflict, habitat loss, and poaching. Human beings are usually the cause of these problems. But by learning about African animals and their endangered status, you can help protect them.

HOW TO DRAW A LION ART LESSON

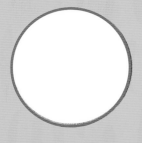

1. Using a pencil and a piece of paper, start by drawing a circle.

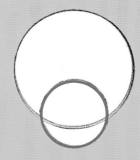

2. Add another circle for the lion's muzzle.

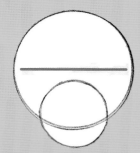

3. Draw a line from side to side. This is where the eyes will be.

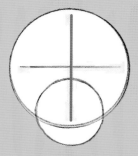

4. Draw another line from top to bottom to show where the lion's nose and mouth will be.

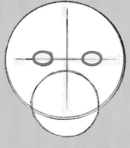

5. Draw two small ovals to give your lion eyes.

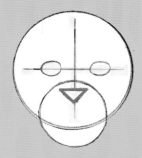

6. Add a triangle for the lion's nose.

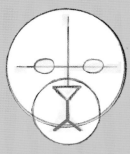

7. Below the triangle, add an upside-down Y for the lion's mouth.

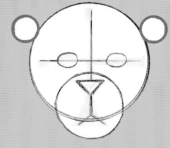

8. Draw two small circles to make his ears.

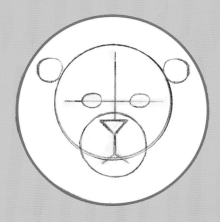

9. Add a large circle on the outside for a mane. OH MY! A lion!

10. It's time to clean up your lion. Use an eraser to remove extra lines.

11. Add some details and furry lines.

And now YOU can paint your lion.

ABOUT THE AUTHORS

In 2014, John Platt visited Tanzania, where he taught marginalized and vulnerable children how to draw and paint. He returned to teach those same students year after year, adding visits to other countries like Kenya and Malawi, where he met even more talented young artists with whom he continues to work. John subsequently founded How to Draw a Lion, Inc., to raise funds to continue the program.

John and Moira Rose Donohue met in Tanzania at the Rift Valley Children's Village in 2017. Moira, a children's writer, was visiting her daughter, who was working at the Children's Village. John and Moira had a creative connection. They knew they wanted to work together to highlight the How to Draw a Lion program and the amazing artwork created by the children, and this book began to take shape.

All the artwork in this book is used with permission of the artists or, if minors, permission of their legal guardians. One hundred percent of the authors' royalties from the sale of this book, including their advance, will be donated to How to Draw a Lion, which continues to support these and future artists in East Africa. Please learn more at drawalion.org. By purchasing this book, you have helped to maintain this program and to celebrate and share the incredible wildlife that is a part of Africa.

For the young artists of Africa

—John

With love to three amazing "children"—Peter, Rose, and RVCV's Musa

—Mama Rose

SLEEPING BEAR PRESS™
2395 South Huron Parkway, Suite 200
Ann Arbor, MI 48104
www.sleepingbearpress.com

Printed and bound in China.

10 9 8 7 6 5 4 3 2 1

Library of Congress Cataloging-in-Publication Data

Names: Platt, John, 1984- author. | Donohue, Moira Rose, author.
Title: Lions & cheetahs & rhinos oh my! : animal artwork by children in sub-Saharan Africa / by John Platt and Moira Rose Donohue ; art by Students from the How to Draw a Lion Program.
Description: Ann Arbor, MI : Sleeping Bear Press, [2020] | Audience: Ages 4-8 | Summary: "Paintings of ten African animals, including lions, zebras, and elephants, are accompanied by nature facts. Each animal portrait is painted by a student from the How to Draw a Lion program, a nonprofit art education program that provides art classes for children in sub-Saharan Africa"— Provided by publisher.
Identifiers: LCCN 2020006364 | ISBN 9781534110540 (hardcover)
Subjects: LCSH: Animals in art—Juvenile literature. | Wildlife art—Juvenile literature. | Drawing—Technique—Juvenile literature.
Classification: LCC NC780 .P53 2020 | DDC 743.6—dc23
LC record available at https://lccn.loc.gov/2020006364